Living in Famous Cities

Living in

Swasti Mitter

Living in Famous Cities

First published in 1980 by
Wayland Publishers Ltd
49 Lansdowne Place, Hove
East Sussex BN3 1HF, England

© Copyright 1980 Wayland Publishers Ltd

ISBN 0 85340 700 2

Phototypeset by Trident Graphics Ltd,
Reigate, Surrey
Printed and bound in the U.K. by
The Pitman Press, Bath

Contents

The biggest city in India

Schoolchildren learn very little about Calcutta, except perhaps about 'the black hole of Calcutta' in their history books. It is, however, an important and fascinating city, full of contrasts.

Calcutta is the largest city in India, with a population of over ten million people, and it is the fourth biggest city in the world. It is the chief port of India, handling almost all the exports and imports of northern India, where 250 million people live. Jute products and tea are the two most important goods which India sells abroad; the port of Calcutta handles 90 per cent of the shipment of these. Also, imported grains, which are vital to feed the people of India in years of drought and bad harvests, are mainly unloaded in this port.

The city lies on the River Hooghly in the delta of the River Ganges, 130 kilometres from the Bay of Bengal. The famous Howrah Bridge over the River Hooghly connects Calcutta to its twin city, also called Howrah. From Howrah, railway lines radiate to all parts of India.

Good sea and rail communications make it easy for Calcutta to maintain its position as India's principal port of trade. It is also one of southern Asia's main commercial and industrial centres. The manufacture of jute into hessian and canvas, and shipbuilding and engineering, are important industries in Calcutta.

When the British ruled India, Calcutta was the capital until 1912, when the Government moved to New Delhi. After Independence in 1947, New Delhi remained the capital of India, and Calcutta is now the capital of West Bengal, one of the twenty-one states that together form the Republic of India today.

Calcutta is the richest city in India, but it also has the largest number of slum dwellers and homeless people. This

A busy street in the centre of Calcutta

4

marked contrast between the rich and the poor, between the elegance and the squalor, is something that deeply upsets most visitors to Calcutta.

This part of the city teems with life

The colonial port and city

On a chance visit to Calcutta, one cannot help noticing some resemblances between the city and London. Chowringhee – the centre of the city – with its hotels and cinemas, its lights and bustle, is a little like Piccadilly Circus. This is not surprising, as Calcutta is a city very British in its origin. Unlike other big cities in northern India, Calcutta did not exist before the British colonization of India nearly 300 years ago.

Calcutta derives its name from Kalikata, one of the three villages which formed the city in 1690. The village was so named because it had a famous temple of Kali, the Hindu Goddess. The Bengalis still call the city Kalikata, using the English version mainly during conversation with foreigners.

The British first came to India in order to trade. The company which was founded for this purpose was called the East India Company. It came to Bengal in 1635. The Company formed its own army so that it could maintain its trading influence over its rivals (Dutch and French traders), and hostile Indian princes. Gradually this army conquered large areas of India.

The Company divided its trading empire into three main provinces: Bengal, Madras and Bombay. In 1690, the British made Calcutta the headquarters of Bengal Province. Calcutta then became the capital of Bengal and the history of the East India Company became the history of the British Empire in India.

The site where Calcutta was founded was unhealthy and was often flooded. The early British inhabitants had great difficulties to overcome. However, trade flourished, and Calcutta grew in size and wealth. Large areas of jungle were cleared, and the present Fort William was erected in 1767 to guard against any invasion of Calcutta from the sea.

Right
Shipping in the River Hooghly when Calcutta was a busy British colonial port

A nineteenth-century view of Calcutta

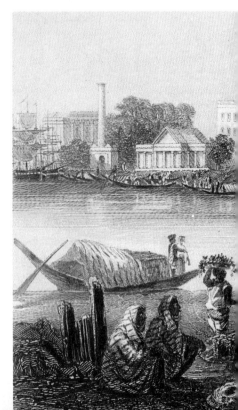

Houses in Calcutta

The British merchants built themselves splendid houses in Calcutta, partly to impress the local people. The style of these buildings came to be known as colonial architecture. The marble Victoria Memorial Hall is a good example. It is situated in the Maidan, a fine grass-covered park which you can see on the colour map. People often go there for a pleasant walk at the end of the day, 'to *eat* the evening air'.

The centre of the city is distinctly British in its planning of the streets and houses. During British rule, this area was mainly reserved for white people and a few rich and westernized Indians. The streets are wide and the flats and houses are designed for Western style living.

The northern part of Calcutta, in contrast, seems much more exotic to Europeans. Rich Indian merchants built themselves great, opulent houses with coloured bricks and huge columns. Around these there are narrow, winding

A typical aristocratic house built in the nineteenth century

Tower blocks are beginning to appear in parts of the city

8

lanes with houses of different sizes and styles. With the pressure of an ever-increasing population many of these houses have been divided into small flats, but some of the splendid houses still exist. The 'Marble Palace', housing great art treasures, is one of them.

The south of Calcutta developed later, at the end of the nineteenth and early twentieth centuries. However, most of these houses are now in a state of decay and property developers are busy demolishing them to build high-rise flats.

Bengalis are artistic people. They decorate their houses in an imaginative way. There is always a little shrine for their gods and goddesses, and flowers are bought every day for them as well as for the living room. Even poor people do their best to use colourful and cheap fabrics to cheer up their surroundings. A friend is always welcome in the house, even when it is not very tidy. Having friends is considered much more important than having time to clean the kitchen floor.

These houses show the great contrast between the homes of rich and poor in Calcutta

The Calcutta summer

At times Calcutta can be very hot and humid. From the middle of March the heat begins to increase, and between then and the start of the monsoon in June the temperature can rise to over 38° Centigrade for days on end. In May it hardly ever falls below 27° Centigrade even at night. The sticky heat can be very uncomfortable. Often the tar on the roads melts, making it difficult to walk.

In the strong haze of the midday sun, lively Calcutta becomes subdued and quiet. Everyone wears white clothes to keep themselves cool, and they go out with black umbrellas for shade. Even the policemen who try to sort out the chaotic traffic of Calcutta use umbrellas. They have ones with special handles that slot into their belts, so that their arms can remain free. Tired workers and clerks from government offices often rest under a tree in the parks during lunchtime for coolness and comfort. And salesmen do a busy trade serving cool Campa-Cola (an Indian version of Coca-Cola), Fanta, and the milk of green coconuts.

Housewives try to keep their flats and houses cool by drawing blinds over the windows during the day. Rich people use air-coolers and air-conditioners or electric fans to make their houses comfortable. But poor people, slum dwellers or families living on the pavement, use fans made out of palm leaves. An exhausted labourer or rickshaw-puller sleeping soundly in the cool porch of a grand house, is a common sight at midday. School holidays last for eight weeks during summer because it is impossible to concentrate on studies in such heat. The high humidity causes people to become drenched with sweat.

It is not difficult to understand why the people of Calcutta are so fond of evening walks. Often the whole family dress up for an evening walk on the bank of the river Ganges, where they can enjoy cool sea breezes.

The sun beats down on these river craft moored in the Hooghley

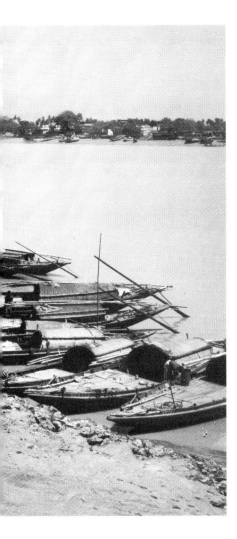

The policeman keeps cool in the extreme heat of summer

Monsoon and winter

The monsoon usually breaks at the beginning of June. The temperature drops, giving joyous relief to everyone. People run out into the streaming rain with sheer pleasure to be cool at last.

Unfortunately the drainage system in Calcutta is rather out-of-date and not always adequate to cope with the monsoon rain. If the rainfall lasts longer than twenty minutes or so, the city becomes completely flooded. Buses, cars and trains come to a stop and the only way to get about is to wade through the knee-high water.

One way of travelling during the monsoon period is to take a rickshaw, which is a small two-wheeled carriage drawn by one or two men called rickshawallahs. Rickshaws can carry two passengers or sometimes more. Being a rickshawallah is not a very pleasant or easy way of earning money. Most of them are very poor, but they are able to charge their passengers two to three times the normal rate during the monsoon period, so they certainly welcome the heavy rainfall of the monsoon.

Winter is the most pleasant time in Calcutta. Between September and February, the weather is quite cool, the sun is mild, and people wear colourful clothes. There is hardly ever any need to heat the house, and this is the only time when the people of Calcutta can enjoy going out in the sun. Winter is also the time of carnivals and festivals, including *Durga Puja*, the biggest Hindu festival of all, when the entire city celebrates for four days. Children have lots of fun then, and are given presents of new clothes.

Water is precious and tanks are often stored on roofs

Opposite
Children wade through the street flooded by monsoon rain

Calcutta

The great waterway of the River Hooghly has made Calcutta an important port and industrial centre. Howrah Bridge links it to Howrah on the opposite bank where the famous Botanical Gardens are situated. South of the Bridge is the bustling port. In the centre of Calcutta is the Maidan, once a fort but now providing an open green space for thousands of people. It contains a zoo and gardens. The imposing Victoria Memorial is a fine museum and all around are splendid houses built by British merchants. To the north are opulent palaces and homes belonging to the wealthy. But vast areas of poor housing cover the south. New homes are being built for thousands of people who have nowhere to live but the streets.

This picture-map shows what Calcutta might look like if you were flying overhead but it cannot show everything as a real map would and is not drawn to scale.

Docks

HOOGH

Zoo

Fort
William

Ed
Gard

MAIDAN

Victoria
Memorial

Och
Mo

CHOWRINGHEE

Indian Museum

Kali Temple

PARK STREET

Birla
Academy

. C A L C

Lakes

Mother Theresa's
Mission of Charity

Sealdah
Station

Marsh

Beliaghata Canal

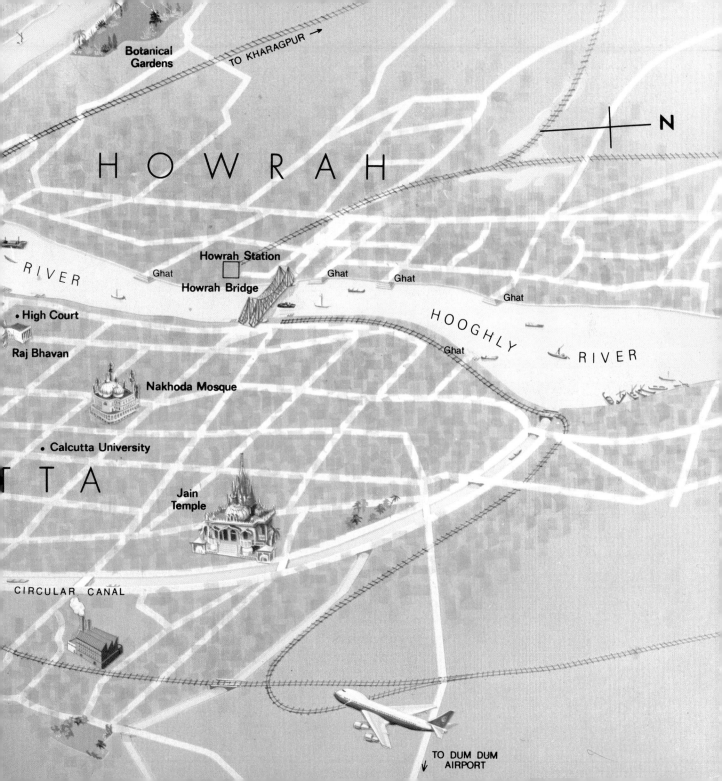

Botanical
Gardens

TO KHARAGPUR →

N

H O W R A H

RIVER

Ghat

Howrah Station

Howrah Bridge

Ghat

Ghat

Ghat

• High Court

Raj Bhavan

HOOGHLY RIVER

Ghat

Nakhoda Mosque

Ghat

• Calcutta University

T T A

Jain
Temple

CIRCULAR CANAL

TO DUM DUM
AIRPORT
↓

Rickshaws are the most dependable means of transport in Calcutta

Transport

Travelling by bus or tram in Calcutta is rather a risky adventure. A bus which is built to carry forty or fifty passengers regularly carries around 200 or more, especially during rush hours. People hang from the roof, doors and windows of the buses, and one has to learn the trick of getting into and out of a bus in which people are packed like sardines. Although it looks terrifying, the people of Calcutta are generally skilful at doing this. Even young children push their way out of the crowds without serious mishaps.

There are several types of buses in Calcutta and they are all very cheap. There are state-owned public buses where one can travel 16 km (ten miles) for less than ten pence. The passengers hanging from the roof-top normally dodge paying the fare. There are de luxe versions of the public buses; they are not luxurious at all and often rattle a lot. But they do not take an unlimited number of passengers, and they charge higher fares. There are also colourful private buses which have names such as 'Punjab Mail' or 'Beauty Queen'. Trams have two carriages, are as crowded as the public buses, and are run by electricity. There is a great feeling of co-operation among the passengers in a bus or tram. Men gladly vacate seats for the elderly, for women and for children, and there are also special seats reserved for women. People joke among themselves to make such crowded journeys bearable.

Deaths from road accidents are far fewer in Calcutta than in European countries. This is mainly because it is difficult to drive in Calcutta streets at any speed. Roads are filled with rickshaws, pedestrians, dogs, cats, and even sleeping bullocks and holy Hindu cows. Cows are sacred animals to the Hindus and they are allowed to roam freely in the streets. Drivers are very careful not to run any of them over.

Jostling crowds cram into buses and taxis on their way home from work

The sacred Hindu cow rests undisturbed on the pavement

Poverty and squalor

Calcutta is often described as a 'nightmare city' by outsiders. The city is littered with garbage. In places, the rubbish piles up to form a series of heaps which obstruct the traffic and the pedestrians. The stench can become overpowering.

Many households have a middle-class breadwinner, and enjoy a modest but graceful standard of living. Things like refrigerators, televisions, and tape-recorders still have some novelty for most Bengalis, and they find great pleasure in acquiring them.

However, life is not very secure for anyone who is not really rich. There is no unemployment benefit, social security, or National Health Service. For the poor, the unemployed or the sick, life is bleak and frightening.

Thousands of families live next to piles of rubbish on the pavement, mother cooking the midday meal, children playing with the hose-water, and the older children picking through the garbage to find something to sell in the market. Often they are poor peasants who have come to Calcutta in search of a job, but cannot find one. If they fail to find jobs, or are too ill to work, they have to beg. The sight of an undernourished baby, sucking the breast of a hungry mother, begging in the street, is heart-breaking, especially in contrast to the signs of rich life close by, which some people can enjoy in this richest city of India.

Many charities try to help the poor in Calcutta. The most famous is the one founded by Mother Teresa, an Albanian Roman Catholic nun, who started her mission with less than five rupees (30 pence) in 1948. She now has many workers helping her. Not a single orphan child is turned away from the *Shishu-Bhawan* – the home for children. And a clean bed is offered to dying beggars so that they feel loved and cared for in the last few days of their lives. She won the Nobel peace prize in 1979.

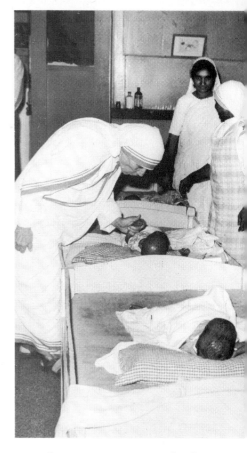

Mother Teresa, Nobel prizewinner, caring for the destitute children of Calcutta

Opposite
Mother prepares a meal on a Calcutta pavement with the baby at her breast

19

Population and pollution

Many of Calcutta's problems are caused by the rapid increase in population which has occurred during the last twenty or thirty years. There are three reasons for this.

In 1947 the province of Bengal was divided in half. The eastern part became East Pakistan (now Bangladesh), an independent state for the Muslims of Bengal. The western part became a Hindu state, with Calcutta as its capital. Millions of Hindu refugees fled from East Bengal to Calcutta in fear of riots. These refugees swelled the population of Calcutta from around 3 million in 1947 to nearly 4 million by 1953. Shanty towns and slums became a common sight near Sealdah, the second biggest railway station in Calcutta, where train-loads of Hindu refugees arrived. The second reason is that thousands of people come each year

Rubbish is a problem in Calcutta; thousands of tons are dumped in the streets every day

Some people live all their lives on the pavement, like this family with all their worldly belongings

20

in search of food, jobs, shelter and government aid. The third reason is that there is such a high death rate! This makes poor people want to have a large family to make sure that they have at least one surviving male child to look after them in their old age. There is no old age pension in Calcutta.

This large expansion of the population has a bad effect on the city. At one time Calcutta was known as the 'City of Gardens', and the 'City of Palaces'. But now it is impossible to find any green space except for a few parks, which become sleeping places for homeless people. Beautiful buildings house too many people and dwindle into a state of decay. People cook in the streets with coal and cakes of fuel made out of baked cow dung. The stale smell and the smoke hang heavily in the evening air, especially in winter. Visitors who are not used to the polluted air often suffer from bronchial troubles.

These roadside shanties are the only homes which many people will ever know

Family life

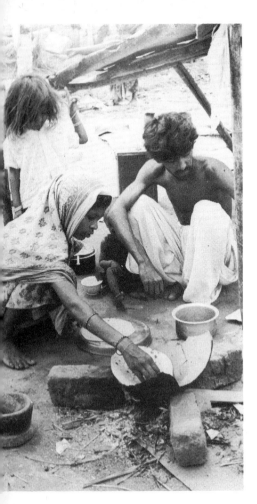

Family life carries on quite happily on the pavements

Life in Calcutta, however, is not all bleak and full of horrors. In spite of hardship, people in the city keep a sense of humour and gaiety, and appreciate any pleasures which life has to offer.

Family life is the greatest source of joy and comfort in Calcutta, as elsewhere in India. Children are pampered and cuddled. Life revolves around the needs of the children in the family. Father goes out in the morning to do the shopping so that his sons and daughters can have their favourite fish for lunch before they go to school. Mother keeps busy with the housework, and helps the children with their homework. Parents lay plans for their children's holidays, careers and even marriage.

In return, children are expected to be respectful to their parents, to obey their orders without much argument, and to look after them in their old age.

Older people in Calcutta have a much more dignified life than in the West. People would never think of sending their parents to 'old people's homes'. Grandparents have a lot of authority in the family, and even a forty-year-old son will ask his father's permission before buying a new car or having a holiday trip abroad.

The 'family' includes the extended family of uncles and aunts. Important occasions such as weddings or name-giving ceremonies will bring all the extended family together. And it is always a joyous occasion. The loving bond between children and their parents is seen everywhere. A mother on the pavement, begging with the child at her breast, will stop and rest in the shadow of a tree in order to cuddle her baby and to sing a lullaby.

Of course, things are changing slowly. It is quite common to find young couples living away from their parents, because of the needs of their job or because they prefer to

have a life entirely of their own. The number of divorces is rising too, especially among richer families where women are increasingly finding interests and ambitions outside the home.

Grandparents live in the same house and look after the grandchildren – there is no generation gap here

The role of women

Women play a very important role in the family. As a wife and mother, a woman looks after the needs of the family. In return, she receives respect and love. The older she gets the more powerful she becomes – and by the time she is herself a mother-in-law, she controls all aspects of the family's life, loving and at times tyrannizing her daughter-in-law and the grandchildren of the family.

However, a woman's life is not always easy in Calcutta. Parents are happy if the new-born infant is a male, for he is going to be their security in old age. A girl is a bad investment: parents must feed, clothe and educate her, and at the end of it all they have to offer a dowry to get her a good husband. Therefore, although daughters are loved dearly, a family will always feel a certain regret when a girl is born.

In Calcutta, girls are not encouraged to find their own husbands. It is the duty of the parents to find a husband for their daughters who belongs to the same caste and economic class. If the girl is not pretty, the dowry may have

This woman, from a privileged home, works in publishing

Not all women are so lucky. This young girl is a servant

Some women make it to the top. This woman is a leading lawyer in Calcutta

to be a large one. *The Statesman* – the most distinguished newspaper in Calcutta – publishes a whole page giving details of prospective brides and grooms including their education, social class, caste, age, and appearance (naturally they are always described as handsome or beautiful). Parents often look through this to find the right boy or girl.

Women, especially the educated, are now protesting against the injustice of the dowry system. As they are taking up more important work outside their home, their protests are becoming more effective. It takes time to change any society, but changes can already be seen in Calcutta. There are a number of organizations trying to improve the situation for women both at home and at work.

Richer families usually encourage their daughters to have the same education as their sons and there are women engineers, doctors, professors, judges and politicians.

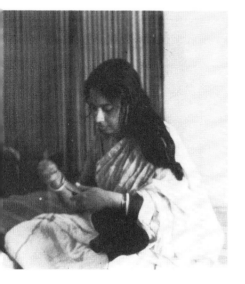

This woman is an accomplished designer of clothes

Recreation and entertainment

People queue up in the midday sun for a seat in the cinema

Calcutta is not a paradise for tourists. But it has a lot to offer to those who live there. In spite of all the squalor, it is filled with the joy of life. There are film shows, plays and children's theatres in all quarters of Calcutta. They are always attended by a large number of people.

Films are an obsession with Bengalis. Even in the midday sun of May, there will be mile-long queues in front of nearly every cinema. Parents always take their children to see a film because there are no 'AA' or 'X' certificates. The censorship is very strict, so most films do not show scenes which are not suitable for children.

Calcutta has produced some of the best film directors in the world. Satyajit Ray is the most famous. His films are known for their great human sympathy and understanding. Calcutta also has a large number of theatre groups, who often stage powerful plays with political messages.

Television is new to Calcutta. It is in black and white only, and immensely popular. But people still rush to cinemas to see the latest film.

Music festivals are also important events in Calcutta life. They start in the evening, continue all night, and finish in mid-morning. Music lovers come with their children, and enjoy themselves just as at pop-festivals in the West.

In Calcutta, there is a great deal of interest in European films and music. There are film clubs which show the best films from Europe and America. People buy records of Beethoven and Bach as enthusiastically as they buy records of Ravi Shankar playing the sitar. Pop records are displayed in music shops beside those of famous Bengali singers.

Football and cricket are the two most popular sports in Calcutta. Children are seen playing cricket everywhere – even on the pavements. The Test players from home and abroad get treatment similar to that of royalty or film stars.

Pavement children play
happily in water from a
hydrant

Father and
father-in-law argue over
the bride's dowry in
this contemporary play

Arts and literature

Most people in Calcutta speak Bengali, and they are very proud of their culture and artistic tradition. The enthusiasm of Bengalis for art has earned them the half-respectful, half-comical title of 'Babus' meaning 'Gentle' men, from other Indians.

People in Calcutta like to read books. This is obvious if one strolls around the streets. There are bookshops everywhere. In many areas there are bookstalls on the pavements selling new and secondhand books.

Publishers are very active there as well. A large number of books and magazines are published every week and there is no shortage of readers. There are always people ready to buy political magazines and newspapers, as Bengalis are very keen on discussing politics. Calcutta has a thriving tradition of literature. The Bengali poet Tagore was the first non-European to receive the Nobel prize for literature (1913), and there are many modern Bengali writers.

As for painting and sculpture, Bengalis are rightly proud of their contribution. Calcutta Art School has produced teachers who have deeply influenced the modern Indian movements in painting and art. In the Academy of Fine Arts, a great gallery for Indian Art, children get expert lessons in painting and sculpture. Unfortunately, children from poor families cannot attend these, as the fees are beyond their means.

But poor children can be creative too. Images of gods and goddesses are made out of clay and the families who make them are by no means rich. The son is trained by his father and the art of modelling and painting images runs in the family. The folk arts of Calcutta are a lively tradition and are displayed in calendars and other publications.

This artist paints portraits of well-known figures

Opposite
Book-stalls in Calcutta

28

Museums and Galleries

There are a number of fine museums in Calcutta. The most important one is the Indian Museum. It contains many attractions ranging from items of ancient Indian art and archaeological specimens to the bones of prehistoric animals and natural history subjects. A dazzling collection of tropical butterflies is a favourite display. People come from distant villages to view and marvel at the objects in this museum. So the Bengalis have named it *Jadu-Ghar* or the 'House of Wonders' to express their awe and pleasure.

The Victoria Memorial Hall, built in memory of the British queen, is noted for its collection of objects commemorating the British Empire in India. The Academy of Fine Arts, a modern gallery, contains a fine collection of paintings and sculptures by contemporary artists. Ashutosh Museum, which has a splendid collection of ancient Indian sculptures, is attached to Calcutta University.

On a trip to Calcutta a visit to Gurusaday Museum is always rewarding. This museum collects and preserves folk arts and handicrafts as reminders of the great tradition of popular arts in India, before they disappear in the modern age.

The 'Marble Palace' in North Calcutta is often visited by Indians and foreign tourists. This quaint mansion, built in distinctly European style in the late nineteenth century, stands out in the middle of traditional North Calcutta. This museum also contains a large collection of European paintings and art objects.

The Birla Planetarium was built quite recently and is of great interest both to the people of Calcutta and to foreign tourists, providing spectacular astronomical exhibitions. Children get the greatest delight from visiting the Zoo, which is one of the finest in the East, and a favourite place for picnics.

The Marble Palace, once the home of a wealthy Bengali family, now contains a fine art collection

Opposite
The Victoria Memorial Hall, an example of British colonial architecture, is now a museum

30

Customs and religion

If you should meet a Bengali friend in the street in Calcutta, you would join your hands as if in prayer, and say 'namaskar'. Children touch the feet of their elders to show love and respect on special days, and in return they get an affectionate kiss on the chin. People demonstrate their affection more openly than in the West, and the special Bengali way of embracing a friend is called *kolakuli*.

Hindus form the largest religious group in Calcutta. However, nearly 20 per cent of the population is Muslim. One of the most important buildings in Calcutta is the mosque of Nakhoda Masjid. The prayer during *Id-Mubarak*, the most important Muslim religious event, is an awe-inspiring display of religious chant. Because of their religious beliefs, Hindus do not eat beef and Muslims do not eat pork. Drinking alcohol is frowned upon socially, although

Inside the Jain Temple

A Hindu funeral — it is the Hindu custom to cremate their dead

it is not against the Hindu religion. Young people do not smoke in front of their parents and elders.

There are also Christians in Calcutta and the Armenian Church is a large building in the city. Christmas is a very festive season. Park Street, the most elegant street in Calcutta, is decorated with lights and flowers, and both Christians and non-Christians celebrate by exchanging gifts and cards.

Durga-Puja, the festival of the Hindus, is the most spectacular event of the year. The festival lasts for four days. The whole of Calcutta gets the feel of a carnival – with lights, music and processions. *Durga-Puja* becomes a festival for the whole city, not just for the Hindus. Images of the Goddess Durga are immersed in the sacred Ganges on the fifth day, and the city has a touch of sadness at the end of its happy frenzy.

There is a big community of the Jain faith in Calcutta. The Jain Temple is well known for its exotic style of architecture of pink stone and glittering mirrors.

Bengali women worshipping the Goddess Durga

Food in a Calcutta home

Bengalis take great pleasure in cooking for their friends and visitors. Even if you drop in for a short visit, they will insist on giving you tea and *Rasagulla*, the famous Bengali sweet made of curds.

A typical lunch or dinner in Calcutta is quite elaborate. You start with a slightly bitter vegetable dish. Then you continue with fried vegetables; dahl, which is a dish made from lentils; a fish or meat curry with more vegetables and chutney; and lastly yogurt as a sweet. It is important to have a variety of dishes with distinct tastes for a really successful meal.

Rice is the staple food of the people in Bengal. They eat rice at least once a day, often up to half a kilogramme every day. Fruits and vegetables are in plentiful supply in Calcutta bazaars. These include different kinds of mangoes

A fish seller in the bazaar – his special knife is for cutting fish

A family meal in a middle-class home

Buying rice from the open market in South Calcutta

and other exotic fruits, and there are apples and pears as well. Cauliflowers, cabbages and other vegetables common in the West are available, and there are also many kinds which are normally not found except in the East.

Bengalis love fish and often eat it every day. There are about seventy varieties of fish in the market. Some, such as prawns or lobsters, are expensive and are bought only for special occasions. And you have not lived in Calcutta if you have not tasted *Hilsa* – the pride and joy of Bengalis. Fishermen in Bengal compose songs about the silvery beauty of the *Hilsa* which they catch in their nets.

All kinds of sweets are made out of milk and curds. *Payesh*, a kind of rice pudding with saffron and almonds, is the traditional sweet to celebrate a child's birthday.

A Bengali bride dressed in her wedding sari and surrounded by traditional decorations

The way people eat, dress and live

Most people eat sitting on a mat or a wooden block, and the plates and cups are made of stainless steel or brass. Bengalis eat with their fingers, and vegetables, meat and fish are sliced thinly to make them easy to eat. People are expected to wash their hands and mouth every time they eat, so it is not surprising that most Bengalis have good teeth.

Women wear saris with a tightly fitting blouse. Young women usually wear colourful saris, wearing white only when it is very hot or when they are in mourning. For her wedding, a girl is expected to wear a flaming red sari, embroidered with real gold or silver thread. Jewellery is an essential part of dressing up and parents save up to buy gold and silver jewellery for their daughter to make her look like a queen, at least for her wedding night. Widows wear white saris all the time and do not wear bangles. Young girls wear jeans and western-style dresses, but they are expected to wear saris by the time they are in their mid-teens.

It is customary for women to have a 'tip', a red mark on their forehead, unless they are widows. It symbolizes happiness and well-being, and is not a caste-mark as many westerners think. Girls wear 'tips' of other colours as well, to match their saris, and they look very attractive.

Men wear a 'dhoti', a male version of a sari. It is always white, and they wear a loose shirt on top. However, some businessmen like to wear western-style clothes. Teenage boys in fashionable areas of Calcutta like to wear 'Levi' or 'Wrangler' jeans.

Homes are very expensive in Calcutta and only really wealthy people own a big house. Often families live in

The time-honoured leisurely way of life beside the River Hooghly

The relaxed atmosphere of an affluent home. Film director Satyajit Ray finds time to talk to guests

small flats, and children do not have a room of their own. Even in a big house, they sleep with their parents. Beds are big, taking up the whole room, and in the daytime, friends will come and sit on the bed for a gossip!

Shopping

Shopping is great fun in Calcutta. Shops do not close at 5.30 p.m. In fact, the shopping areas become especially busy after the schools, colleges and offices are closed. It is cooler in the evening, the lights are on, people wear attractive clothes to go out, and the shopping districts have a festive feeling. There are shops selling clothes and fabrics where women will go in a group, to see the saris and dresses, and bargain about the price. The shopkeepers are always welcoming and like to chat with the customers on all kinds of topics, such as weather and politics. Also there are stalls on the pavement selling cheaper goods which are often run by refugees from Bangladesh, and offer goods at bargain prices.

The most impressive shopping centres are the bazaars. There are at least eight main bazaars in Calcutta. There is little chance for a leisurely stroll. You haggle and weigh, decide on the price, take your things, and move on to the next stall. But there is always a smile from the shopkeeper and he is bound to ask after your children's good health or the state of your new house. If you are a regular customer, he will even give you goods on credit — so long as you do not expect this too often. This kind of human touch and sense of sympathy make Calcutta a heartening place to live in, even in the middle of poverty and squalor.

Shopping does not only mean buying things necessary for living; at the end of shopping men buy garlands of flowers for their wives or for the family gods. There is also the pleasure of chewing *Paan* (a leaf which makes your lips red and your mouth feel fresh) in a friendly group. No one need be lonely in Calcutta — you are bound to find someone to talk to in a paan-shop or at a tea-stall. Shopping is a really communal activity in the city.

A pavement vendor displays his wares

A customer examines the quality of the potatoes before she decides to buy

38

Schools

Most middle-class children go to fee-paying schools in Calcutta, and some schools can be very expensive. It is not compulsory for children to go to school and it is up to the parents to decide about their education.

Poor parents often cannot send their children to school at all. At the age of eight or nine their children are likely to take up jobs as servants, cook's assistants, or shoeshine boys. Any income is welcomed to supplement meagre family earnings, so many parents encourage their children to work rather than go to school. There are some primary schools run by the Calcutta Corporation, which are free schools for young children up to ten years old. They are run both in the mornings and in the evenings, so that poor children who have to work can attend them, and learn to read and write.

All other schools cater for the richer families. There are far more children than school places, so the best schools can be very selective. In the famous schools of Calcutta, for every hundred places, at least a thousand children at the age of six sit a stiff examination. So children have to work very hard even from their earliest years. Opportunities are limited in Calcutta, and parents know that their sons and daughters will have a better chance of success if they are good at their studies. They feel very proud when their children do well in examinations.

The pressure to do well is at times too hard for the children. They envy the free atmosphere of some Western schools where each child is allowed to develop at his or her own pace. However, the bright children do learn a lot under the pressure, and often grow up to make important contributions to science, arts and literature. School life can, however, be tough for those who are not so able.

Children taking part in a school painting competition

A typical classroom in Calcutta

Not all children can aspire to higher education and only a few can hope to get into this prestigious college

42

A typical school day

Children begin school at about 11.0 in the morning. They sometimes do some of their homework before they set off for school. By 9.0 a.m. they will be ready to sit down to a full breakfast, while Mother is busy preparing *tiffin* – a packed meal of savoury snacks and fruits for midday break in school.

Schools have fairly long hours and children are expected to work hard. Breaks for games and sports, and facilities for music and art are rather limited. Children have very little relief from studying, and learning. The break for *tiffin* is therefore something to look forward to. This lasts for nearly an hour, and boys and girls find an outlet for their energy by playing games in the school playground.

The most expensive schools in Calcutta are run by Jesuit missionaries. Children from rich families attend these schools where English is taught as much as Bengali, from a very early age. The children who go to these schools learn to read, write and talk English as fluently as English-speaking children, although with an Indian accent.

Children who go to other schools are mainly taught Bengali. Although they start to learn English at the age of eight or nine, they are not taught so rigorously, but most can read and write some kind of English. Bright children are often able to speak fluent English by the last year of their schooling. However, they often feel shy of speaking English as they do not have very much opportunity for conversation in the language.

School finishes at 4.30 p.m. Some children return home by school bus, but it is an expensive form of travel and not all parents can afford this luxury. However, whatever may be the transport, there is always a mother waiting for the tired children with delicious tea.

Waiting for the school bus in the morning

Opposite
Children in the playground of a Calcutta kindergarten

Politics

A poster in West Bengal during a General Election

The contrast between the rich and the poor is so great in Calcutta that all sensitive and intelligent people feel a sense of injustice. Bright children in schools, colleges and universities try to think about the causes of this inequality, so that they can attempt to change this unequal society when they grow up.

Politics is therefore one of the greatest passions among young people in Calcutta. Most good films, plays, and writings show keen social awareness and often deep commitment to the problems of India. Many magazines are devoted only to political subjects.

Ideals of communism seem attractive, especially to young people. They see in these a message of hope for justice and equality and therefore communism captures the imagination and idealism of those who want to help the poor and the unemployed. There are two major communist parties in Calcutta, as well as smaller socialist parties so it is not easy for people to decide which one to join.

One of the reasons why people think about politics so much is that there are large numbers of unemployed. These are not only among the uneducated, but even among highly educated and skilled people. Nearly 50 per cent of the graduates have hardly any hope of a job when they leave university, and a large number never find a job or livelihood at all. In a society where there are no social security benefits, such a prospect can be frightening. Therefore many people feel that the only way to bring justice would be to change society completely, provide jobs for everybody, and narrow the difference between the rich and the poor.

No political party has yet provided a clear plan for achieving this noble, but difficult, goal. Yet the politically thinking people of Calcutta are always busy in the search

44

for a solution. Students and young people take a specially active part in politics. This sometimes results in unrest, riots and student violence.

Calcutta women taking part in a political demonstration

Industry and commerce

Calcutta is always in the news in India because of its importance and its problems. The port of Calcutta handles forty per cent of India's total exports and twenty-five per cent of its total imports. Exports include jute, cotton goods and tea. More than a quarter of India's steel, a third of her coal and almost half of her railway equipment come from West Bengal, making Calcutta a very important industrial centre of India. The country's growth and prosperity depend on the wealth produced in Calcutta and its surrounding areas.

However, the city suffers from the many problems associated with an industrial city. Unemployment and political unrest produce trouble among workers and many working days are lost through strikes. Labour disputes in Calcutta are the worst in India and have led to the closure of a number of factories.

Because of the large amount of industry in the seventy kilometre strip on both sides of the River Hooghly, Calcutta bears the brunt of any economic change in West Bengal. The remaining part of the area is almost entirely rural. The government is trying to spread industry to other districts of West Bengal and, if factories can be built in these rural areas, some of the problems which Calcutta faces may be reduced.

Severe power cuts and crises have contributed to the economic plight of Calcutta. It has not been possible to cope with the rising demand for electricity both at home and in factories. Although government-owned power plants assist the inadequate supply provided by the privately owned Calcutta Electricity Corporation, there are quite often power cuts lasting for six or seven hours at a stretch in the city. These cuts are extremely uncomfortable, especially in the summer, without electric fans and air-

Work in progress on the planned underground railway system for Calcutta

conditioning, and are quite disastrous for factories which have to produce and deliver goods on time. There are ambitious plans to solve this acute power shortage.

The normally busy port lies idle during a strike

Alternative Calcutta

The hope and optimism of the people of Calcutta are apparent in this poster

In recent years there has been a great effort to improve the living standards of the people of Calcutta. A planned city to the east of Calcutta, called Lake Lown, is an attempt to reduce the pressure of the population and all its problems.

Also, a massive network of underground railways is being built. It may take a few years before it is finished, but when it is completed it should make the streets of Calcutta cleaner and less crowded.

There have been attempts to beautify Calcutta by clearing parks and repairing roads. These have been carried out by the Calcutta Metropolitan Development Authority with money provided by the Indian Government and several international agencies. They try to make the physical conditions of living in the city more pleasant and bearable. It is a very difficult task and it would not be fair to expect immediate results. But some improvements to the city can already be seen.

Calcutta, deep as its problems are, is no doomed city. The greatest redeeming feature of the city is the people of Calcutta themselves, who love it and take a great pride in it. In the midst of all their hardships they rightly feel there are many compensations. They also hope for a better future. You can see posters all around Calcutta with messages like this: *Let Calcutta be the pride of Heaven some day.* And it is this hope which keeps the people of this great and incredible city going.

Glossary

Bengal	The western part of the province of Bengal, now in India. Calcutta, the principal city of India is situated in Bengal.
Bengalis	The people who live in Calcutta and in Bangladesh.
Caste or caste system	The system which divides Hindu people into strict hereditary classes, and therefore determines their social position.
Chowringhee	The central district of Calcutta.
Dhoti	The long white garment worn by men in India.
Durga-Puja	The greatest Hindu festival held in Calcutta, which lasts for four days.
East India Company	The British trading company founded in 1600, which came to India in 1635. In 1690 they made Calcutta their headquarters in Bengal.
Hilsa	A fish which is delicious when cooked and a very popular dish with Bengalis.
Id-Mubarak	The most important religious festival in Calcutta.
Jain Faith	A sect of the Hindu religion.
Jute	A plant from which a very strong fibre is made, used for rope, sacks and matting.
Kali	The Hindu goddess of destruction.
Monsoon	The seasonal wind which brings with it very heavy rain. It lasts for three months.
Paan	The leaf of the betel plant, which together with the betel nut, is chewed by people in south-east Asia. Bengalis meet each other in paan-shops where they can chew the leaf and converse.
Rickshaw	A small two-wheeled passenger vehicle, which is drawn by one or two men.
Shishu-Bhawan	The famous home for children founded by Mother Teresa in Calcutta.
Tip	The coloured mark which girls wear on their foreheads. It symbolizes happiness and well-being.

Learn more about Calcutta

Books:

  India by Zaidee Lindsay. (A. and C. Black)
  Indian Crafts and Lore by W. Ben Hunt. (Hamlyn)
  Let's visit India by John C. Caldwell (Burke Publishing)
  South Asia – Finding out about Geography by Robert
  Clayton and John Miles. (Hart-Davis)
  The Ganges by Gina Douglas. (Wayland)

Other Information sources:

  India Government Tourist Office, 21 New Bond Street, London W.1.
  High Commission for India, India House, Aldwych, London W.C.2.

Picture acknowledgements

The publishers wish to thank the Government of India Tourist Office for permission to use their picture on pages 32–3; the High Commission for India for permission to use their picture on page 31; and Oxfam for permission to use their pictures on pages 21, 22, 42, 49. Other pictures are from Amiya Tarafdar, 13, 16, 20 (upper), 27 (lower), 33, 41 (upper), 43; Keystone Press Agency, 5, 8–9, 40, 47; Mansell Picture Library, 6, 7; Partha Mitter, 4, 8, 19, 20 (lower), 23, 24 (upper and lower), 25 (upper and lower), 26, 27 (upper), 29, 32, 34, 34–5, 36, 37 (lower), 39 (upper and lower), 41 (lower), 44, 45, 46, 48; John Topham, 2–3, 9, 14, 17 (upper and lower), 35, 37 (upper); John Hillelson, 28. Cover picture by Alan Hutchison

The coloured map appearing on pages 14–15 is by Alan Gunston.

Index